Simplify Social Media for Recruiting

The landscape for growing a business has changed dramatically in the past several years. Social media has evolved from a forum for friends and family to stay connected to a critical business tool. What I've learned is that if you are starting a new venture or staffing an existing one and you're not fully engaged with a social media strategy, you're going to be left behind by the competition. As an entrepreneur who has launched several successful businesses, my appreciation for leveraging social media and all of its benefits has been high, but I lacked the fundamental knowledge of how to do it. That was before I read, "*Simplify Social Media for Recruiting – A Step-by Step Handbook for Implementing Social Media.*" In a clear, concise and easy to follow style, this book has taken my level of understanding and awareness of how to implement an effective social media strategy to a whole new level. Thank you Eileen and Kathy!

Tom Wimer, President & CEO, Axeo

From the most technically illiterate to the most technically savvy recruiter, this book empowers recruiters to learn how social media is changing the dynamics of recruiting today.

Meghana Dave, Advanced Recruiting Services

SIMPLIFY
Social Media
for Recruiting

A Step-by-Step Handbook for
Implementing Social Media

Kathy Mulder-Williamson
and **Eileen M. Taylor**

iUniverse, Inc.
Bloomington

SIMPLIFY SOCIAL MEDIA FOR RECRUITING
A STEP-BY-STEP HANDBOOK FOR IMPLEMENTING SOCIAL MEDIA

iUniverse books may be ordered through booksellers or by contacting:
iUniverse
1663 Liberty Drive
Bloomington, IN 47403
www.iuniverse.com
1-800-Authors (1-800-288-4677)

ISBN: 978-1-4759-8076-9 (sc)
ISBN: 978-1-4759-8075-2 (hc)
ISBN: 978-1-4759-8077-6 (e)

Library of Congress Control Number: 2013904259

Printed in the United States of America

iUniverse rev. date: 4/9/2013

Contents

Preface _____ ix
About the authors

Introduction to the Handbook _____ 1
What's in it for you?

Getting Started _____ 5
How to use this handbook

What Is Social Media? _____ 7
A simple introduction for the beginner

An Overview of Frequently Used Social Media Sites _____ 13
Twitter, Facebook, LinkedIn, and Google+

How to Create Your Social Media Sites _____ 29
Step-by-step instructions for setting up Twitter,
Facebook, LinkedIn, and Google+

Tools and Tips to Maximize Your Use of Social Media _____ 57
Get it done easier, faster, and more efficiently

Applicant Tracking System _____ 71
Why it is important to use in conjunction with social media

Strategy and Policy/Guidelines _____ 77
Guidance on developing a social media strategy and policy/guidelines

‼ Social Media Warnings _____ 83
Guarding against the risks associated with social media

Conclusion _____ 87

Glossary _____ 89
Definitions of popular terms used in social media

Preface

Afte Eileen M. Taylor hired Kathy Mulder-Williamson to provide recruitment services to her firm, she was surprised to learn the number of passive and hard-to-find candidates Kathy was sourcing using the Internet, long before social media became a household word. Eileen and Kathy realized the power of Internet tools, and together they explored and tested different avenues for recruiting, discovering the potential of LinkedIn before it became the sourcing tool it is today. They created time-saving techniques using Internet-based tools for sourcing candidates, posting job opportunities, and marketing on LinkedIn, Twitter, and Facebook.

Eileen and Kathy decided to partner and write this handbook, sharing their social media passion and knowledge and helping recruiters and human resource professionals avoid wasting the countless hours it takes to learn the tips and tools of social media.

It is through this shared experience that hyrebuzz, llc, was born, offering consulting services in social media, recruitment, and training. Hyrebuzz works with employers to maximize social media and traditional methods to source candidates and to brand and market their organization as an employer of choice.

Kathy Mulder-Williamson owns a business providing recruitment consulting services in the Washington, DC, metropolitan area. She is experienced at sourcing and recruiting in the United States, Asia, and Europe. Kathy has a keen interest in technology and is continually researching and incorporating future trends in recruiting. She leverages the growing and evolving Internet and social media tools to source candidates and publicize job opportunities. Kathy has been using LinkedIn to recruit since it was in its infancy, in 2004, and was on the beta-testing team for one of the first Internet job boards to hit the market. It is Kathy's passion—and somewhat of an obsession—to tirelessly research and share her knowledge of these tools with clients and colleagues.

Eileen M. Taylor, SPHR, is a business executive specializing in human resource consulting. She is a lifelong writer/editor by avocation. Eileen's career in human resources spans commercial, nonprofit, and government industries. Managing recruiting, often with little or no budget, Eileen searched for inventive low-cost ways to publicize job openings and became an advocate of using the Internet when she first discovered Craig's List. It is through her association with Kathy that she broadened her knowledge of using the Internet to support human resource activities. As a teacher of other human resource professionals, Eileen realized that the industry needed a handbook that would simplify the business use of social media.

Introduction to the Handbook

What's in it for you?

Your business is only as great as your people. You've got a unique product or an outstanding service; you've got the infrastructure to deliver it; you're ready to take your organization to the next level. So how do you find the best people to get you there? Where are candidates hiding? These days, the answer is simple: they're online, just like everyone else! But finding that one qualified candidate among the millions of users who are telling the world who they are and what they can do via Facebook, Twitter, LinkedIn, and dozens of other social networking sites can seem like searching for that proverbial needle in the haystack. Where do you even begin?

We at hyrebuzz have spent countless hours seeking to leverage the most easy-to-use, powerful, inexpensive, and all-around best social networking tools to help with recruiting, and we've written this handbook to share what we've learned with you. If you are recruiting in the twenty-first century, you need to use social networks to your advantage. By using social media, you will find that you can

- enhance your organization's brand recognition as an employer of choice;
- identify qualified candidates more quickly, efficiently, and inexpensively than ever before;
- recruit passive applicants who otherwise would not know of your openings—there are more than *one hundred million* profiles on the large social media sites;

- target applicants based on such characteristics as geographical location, education, and skills;
- net more qualified candidates in less time;
- make it easier for candidates to contact you and apply for a job;
- obtain more information about a candidate than what is on a résumé or curriculum vitae;
- compare what is on a candidate's résumé or curriculum vitae to what is on his or her social media pages; and
- better screen for organizational and cultural fit *before the interview.*

As you well know, filling positions isn't a one-way street. Social networks won't just help you choose the right people; they'll help ensure that the right people choose *you.* You'll make a good first impression on those candidates whom you interview by showing them that your organization uses the most efficient and contemporary tools available.

While social networks are relatively simple to use and require no cash outlay to access, they do require time and energy. And if you choose to use social networks to their best possible advantage, it will cost you money to pay someone to maintain the networks or even enhance them through design and multimedia. Each site is different, and weaving them together effectively requires that you understand how to leverage the many and varied tools available, even as sites change by the second.

But now you're no longer out to sea in the social media storm. This handbook takes the many options and presents them in a simple, instructional, and easy-to-read format.

As you take the next steps toward online recruiting, stay connected with hyrebuzz. In the ever-evolving social network landscape, there is no way to keep a printed guide current, so we are making updates available through our website: www.hyrebuzz.com. Be a part of keeping us up to the minute! If you have information that others will find useful or questions about the handbook, please share with us.

And know that hyrebuzz goes far beyond our handbook. We're here to expand your recruiting versatility through training, consultation, advice, support, and other resources. If you or your colleagues want to keep expanding on what you've learned from this handbook, visit our website at www.hyrebuzz.com.

So start turning pages—and start finding the best people to fit your organization.

Getting Started

How to use this handbook

You've picked up this handbook because you recognize the value of social media when it comes to recruiting and you want to take greater advantage of this powerful tool.

To help you leverage social media to your organization's advantage, we will show you, step-by-step, how to become a user of the major social networking sites and how to maximize their efficiency and efficacy.

This handbook is straightforward and pared down; **you can read it cover to cover or zero in on the sections that address your specific needs**.

As you proceed through this handbook, you'll find step-by-step instructions for creating social media pages, which appear in the form of step checklists to help you track your progress. To the right of each step checklist is space for you to make notes in advance or as you progress. For instance, you might want to jot down a blog address to include on a social media page or highlight a suggested change to your website that will allow it to sync with your social media page.

Read through all the steps before you begin setting up the social media pages so that you are prepared in advance. By having your digital files and content ready, you can quickly and easily go through all of the steps at one time.

You'll find potential pitfalls in using social media highlighted with this symbol—‼️—so you can take special care to avoid them. We'll use this symbol—$$—to let you know when you have to pay for a service or feature. But don't worry; most of the options we'll discuss are free of charge. You'll also find all the tools and terms specific to social media listed at the back of the handbook in the glossary, which you can refer to as you read and implement the handbook's instructions. And to get started, all you need is a computer and an Internet connection! We'll discuss how you may find that you want to integrate more tools, like an applicant-tracking system, into your online recruiting efforts, but we'll start simple. Just get online, and you're ready to begin.

What Is Social Media?

A simple introduction for the beginner

In this section we'll introduce social media in general. **If you are already familiar with social media, you can skip to the next section**, which will familiarize you with the key social media sites we recommend that you use for recruiting.

We started this book with a bold claim: social media can revolutionize your recruiting results. But what exactly *is* this seemingly magic tool? To quote web analytics expert Avinash Kaushik: "Social media is like teen sex. Everyone wants to do it. Nobody knows how. When it's finally done, there is surprise it's not better."

Social media sites are popular, easy to use, and effective for quick and immediate communication to a broad audience of friends, family, fans, and colleagues.

Social media sites are websites where people who subscribe can communicate and exchange information with each other via the Internet. These websites contain whatever you elect to include, such as demographic, educational, experiential, personal, and organizational information; images and messages about you or your organization; posted messages, blogs, videos, photographs, surveys, games, and links to other sites; and feeds that bring information in from other websites.

When you "post" information on a social media site, the information can be viewed by those with whom you choose to connect by following, friending, and linking—as long as your connections visit the site. So that you can limit who is able to see various types of information you share on a social media site, your connections each have settings that allow you to define who can see parts of, or all of, your page.

While many social media sites provide free basic membership when you sign up and create a username and password, social media sites often offer "extras" for a fee. These extras tend to be low in cost but are not necessary for use of the site. For example, on LinkedIn you can advertise by paying for LinkedIn ads; or on Facebook you can buy Facebook credits, which can be used to send "gifts" or to purchase applications and games.

When you use social media, communicating with people and organizations you know who also use social media becomes very simple: when you post a photograph, greeting, well wish, update, news, or other information, it can be seen immediately by those with whom you have chosen to connect. Here's an example: If you have a Facebook account, you can share photographs of a trip by creating a photograph album and uploading your favorite photographs to it (which is *very* easy and intuitive to do). Everyone whom you have "friended" on Facebook can log in and see those photographs at any time, making it easier to stay in touch regardless of how near or far you are from your "friends."

‼ Social media sites can absorb an incredible amount of your time, if you let them. Like reality television and soap operas, social media can suck you in before you know it!

Since there are countless social media sites, and the number increases by the minute, we are going to focus on the small segment of the ever-expanding social media universe that is particularly useful for recruiting. These sites are Twitter, Facebook, LinkedIn, and Google+.

Decoding the lingo can be frustrating, so before we dive into the nitty-gritty of these four sites, here are some common terms that you'll see come up again and again. For a complete list, turn to the back of this handbook.

- **avatar:** An avatar is a graphical image that social media users use to represent themselves rather than using an actual personal photograph.

- **blog:** A shortening of the term "web log," which refers to an electronic journal or written conversation on a website, usually generated by someone who wants to share their activities and thoughts or engage in a virtual debate. In the movie *Julie and Julia,* the character Julie writes a daily blog about her experiences as she hones her French cooking skills recipe by recipe from a Julia Child cookbook. When her blog gets discovered and gains a following, she gains notoriety. You can read and respond to someone else's blog. Each written blog entry is dated and appears in reverse chronological order.

- **follower:** On Twitter, if you want to read all of the Tweets with Twitter of another Twitter user, you must become a "follower" of theirs. When you "follow" a Twitter account holder, their Tweets with Twitter will post on your Twitter page, and when another Twitter account holder "follows" you, your Tweets with Twitter will appear on their Twitter page.

- **hashtag:** In order for you to be able to search for Tweets with Twitter about a certain subject, Tweets with Twitter have to contain a key reference word called a "hashtag." This is a word that has a hash mark as its first character, like "#socialmedia." If you searched Twitter for #socialmedia, you would see Tweets with Twitter that contain the #socialmedia hashtag.

- **link:** A person to whom you are connected via LinkedIn. You can stay connected with your links and follow their advancements and changes in professional activities.

- **post:** A message that appears on a social media site, where it can be viewed by others. Also a verb, "to post": to share on a social media site.

- **retweet:** A Tweet that you post on Twitter to share with your followers and that one of your followers then reposts to their followers. If one of your Tweets with Twitter gets retweeted, your Twitter username will appear beside it to indicate who originated the Tweet.

- **RSS feed:** An acronym for rich site summary, also called really simple syndication. RSS feeds allow you to subscribe to content on blogs and other social media so that you can continually receive notice of new posts via a running feed.

- **search engine:** A tool you can use to search for information on the World Wide Web and FTP servers. Google is today's most widely used search engine. When you enter a search topic, the search engine combs the Internet for sites that reference the topic and lists the web pages and files it finds in order from the most to the least precise match. Each item the search engine finds and lists is called a "hit."

- **tag:** A keyword in or attached to a blog post, bookmark, photograph, or other item. Tags enable you to find what you want when searching the web.

- **Tweet:** A message posted on Twitter by a Twitter account holder. Tweets with Twitter have a 140-character limit.

- **XML:** An acronym for extensible markup language, a set of rules for encoding documents in a machine-readable form, like html. XML formats documents, making them simple and usable over the Internet.

Ready to go to the next step?

Okay, then quiz yourself to see how much you have retained ...

1. In order to use a social media site, you must become a
____.
2. True or false: An RSS feed allows you to subscribe to a blog.
3. The overarching purpose of social media is to:
    a. Match up people who want to go on dates.
    b. Facilitate communication between members.
    c. Create groups for people who want to socialize.

Answers: 1. member or user; 2. true; 3. b

Now let's move on to an overview of a few key social media sites you can easily and inexpensively use for recruiting.

An Overview of Frequently Used Social Media Sites

Twitter, Facebook, LinkedIn, and Google+

If you are already familiar with Twitter, Facebook, LinkedIn, and Google+, you may want to skip to the next section, where we get into the specifics of how to create profiles for your organization on each of these sites.

In this section, we'll zero in on Twitter, Facebook, LinkedIn, and Google+, four widely used social media sites that we recommend you use for recruiting. Social media is such a powerful tool because, using sites like these, you can spread the word about job opportunities very quickly and at only the cost of your time. The four sites hyrebuzz has chosen to spotlight have become so ubiquitous that the sites are almost mandatory. If, for example, college recruiting is part of your recruitment strategy, you may be expected to provide your organization's social media page URLs when you register on the school's career website. Once you become familiar with how to use social media to recruit, it will take very little of your time to post job information and, with one posting, broadcast the job across multiple sites.

Twitter

What is Twitter? Twitter, pictured in the accompanying screenshot image, is a social media site designed to allow users to publish quick, brief messages via the Internet. When you set up an account and become a Twitter user, you can select other Twitter users you want to "follow" and others can elect to "follow" you. When you log in to your Twitter account, you will see the most recent Tweets with Twitter of all those you follow. You'll also have a profile page, which displays your username (Twitter usernames are preceded by the @ symbol), a 160-character bio, a profile picture or "avatar," and a link to a web page or blog, if you have one. Profile pictures are compressed to a very small size and appear to the left of published Tweets with Twitter along with the Tweeter's username so that followers know who posted. Some can be difficult to see, as you'll notice if you visit Nelson Mandela's Twitter page, https://twitter .com/NelsonMandela; the logos and long words do not display well. By contrast, you can see that the Sydney Symphony Orchestra's https://twitter.com/sydsmph Twitter page logo shows well when it is compressed, even though it is larger. Check out the accompanying screenshot of the Recruiter Dynamics Twitter page at https://twitter .com/Recruitdynamics.

Since its inception, Twitter has experienced explosive growth, with over four hundred million views per month and twenty-seven million Tweets with Twitter per day. Employees and consultants use it when searching for organizations to work for—so, shouldn't you be using it to find employees and consultants to work for your organization?

What are Tweets? Tweets are messages you post on Twitter. Tweets with Twitter are limited to 140 characters in length but can contain any information you wish to share with your followers, such as your thoughts and activities, messages you receive from and forward to others, news and information from sources you find interesting, or photographs and ideas. Tweets with Twitter are almost like web-based text messages. Every new Tweet with Twitter you post appears at the top of your Twitter page, with prior Tweets with Twitter appearing below it.

Why Tweet? We Tweet with Twitter to share brief information quickly. Here's an example of what we mean. Picture yourself in the Everglades in Florida. You see two American alligators for the very first time and are so wowed by these amazing creatures that you want to share it with others. All you have to do is snap a picture with your mobile phone, tap the Twitter icon, type in, *"In the Everglades, look @ these spectacular creatures,"* tap the camera icon, select the alligator image from your mobile phone's gallery of photographs, tap "Tweet," and *voila!* Everyone who follows you will see your Tweet with Twitter on their Twitter home page and can admire these amazing creatures. In one minute you have shared your experience with those who follow you—in real time. The same process can apply to your professional needs. You can Tweet with Twitter about a job and include a link to your

American Alligators, Everglades National Park, courtesy of J. David Chafaris, Image Net, Photographer

organization's career page. Let's consider the Sydney Symphony Orchestra, who might Tweet with Twitter, *"Hiring for a Concertmaster, visit our website @* http://www.sydneysymphony.com/shared/documents/jobs/concertmaster/files/4787/Concertmaster.pdf." This costs nothing other than the three minutes it takes to log in to Twitter, enter seven words, and copy and paste the link to their website.

Why get followers? If you Tweet with Twitter, who is going to read it if you don't have followers? If you have a personal Twitter page, you may want to communicate with just your personal circle of friends, relatives, and acquaintances. If your Twitter page represents you as a professional, either as someone who is famous for what you do or as the official "Tweeter" of your organization, you may seek to have millions of followers. You always have the option to block people whom you do not want to follow you. As a professional, you can use your Twitter page to familiarize your followers with the products and services you offer, let your followers know how and where to access them, and gather competitive market intelligence. A performing artist or speaker who gets a following of hundreds of thousands or even millions can Tweet with Twitter dates and locations of performances and appearances and include a link for purchasing tickets, thereby driving larger audiences and ticket sales. By building a following and using techniques to continually increase your followers, you expand the universe of people who learn about your products, services, and job opportunities. If you post interesting, informative, entertaining, relevant, and timely Tweets with Twitter, your followers will retweet you to their followers. Every time a new Twitter user sees a Tweet with Twitter from you that a follower has retweeted, you increase your chances of getting another follower. It takes time and work to build up a Twitter following, and you really do need to Tweet with Twitter often.

‼ Who is real? Because some celebrities have had fans and imposters create Twitter pages with their name and photograph, you might believe that you are seeing a famous person's Twitter page and Tweets with Twitter when really you are not. In order to help you identify which Twitter page is the actual page of the person you want to follow, Twitter offers verification of the identities of users of note. A verified Twitter page displays an icon with a white check mark in the center of a blue circular cloud. If you visit Nelson Mandela's Twitter page using the URL https://twitter.com/NelsonMandela, you will see that his Twitter page has been verified, so you know it is *his* and not that of an imposter.

Facebook

What is Facebook? Facebook is a social media site where friends, family, and colleagues can connect, share photographs and images, meet new people, and discover new organizations. Facebook is more flexible and personal than Twitter because Facebook messages are not limited to 140 characters and because you can include more information about yourself or your organization than on your Twitter page. For example, on Facebook you can include information related to employment, hobbies, products, and services. All of the information you have on your Facebook page will remain there until you remove it. You can upload a single photograph with a posted message or create a photograph album with a whole series of photographs on a single topic or event. Each photograph you upload can have a brief description and the names of the people in the photograph (someone must have a Facebook page in order to be identified, or "tagged," in a picture). You can post messages on your friends' "timelines" (their personal pages) and see their "status updates" (messages, links, and photographs) in the "news feed" on your Facebook home page. In addition, you can create an event, select people you want to invite, and keep track of RSVPs.

According to Facebook, users spend more than seven hundred billion minutes per month on Facebook, and about 50 percent log in to Facebook on any given day.

When you set up an account and become a Facebook user, you can choose other Facebook users you want to "friend," and other Facebook users can "friend" you. Friending must be mutual, so unlike on Twitter, where you can follow someone who is not following you, a Facebook user will not be able to see your timeline until you accept his or her friend request. Once you become Facebook friends with someone, you will see their status updates and photographs in your news feed or timeline. In Facebook, you can protect certain information and images from being seen by everyone by creating different lists and putting your friends in those lists and then designating which list can see what information. This allows you to have a selective audience for images and posts you don't want seen by all of your Facebook friends. One way to do this is to create groups: a *secret* group allows only members to see the group's page, its member list, and what members post; a *closed* group allows anyone to see the group and who's in it, but only members can see posts; and an *open* (public) group allows anyone to see the group, who's in it, and what members post.

While business Facebook accounts are much less interactive than personal accounts and you won't be able to do as much with them as with a personal Facebook page, business Facebook pages are still worth having for recruiting and branding purposes.

Facebook pages include a profile picture or avatar and can include a link to your web page or blog. The profile picture or avatar is compressed to a very small size and appears to the left of Facebook posts. Not all images work well as a profile picture or avatar—visit Andrea Bocelli's Facebook page and see how well you can see the profile picture that appears to the left of his posts, even though the image is small: https://www.facebook.com/NathanPachecoMusic?sk=app_256012207815369#!/pages/Andrea-Bocelli-Italy/141988092496597.

What are posts? Posts, or status updates, are messages you enter in Facebook on your timeline. You can post any information you wish to share with others, such as your thoughts and activities, responses to the posts of others, photographs, and links. Status updates are different from Tweets with Twitter in that Facebook posts are not limited to 140 characters and numerous friends can comment on a status update or "like" it, creating a comment thread below the related post. In addition to updating your status, you can conduct surveys, play games, send greeting cards, and "chat" with friends who are logged in to Facebook, in real time. In addition to posts you generate, you can see a friend's post or uploaded photograph and show that you enjoyed it by simply clicking on the "like" button beneath the post or photograph.

Why post and participate on Facebook? If you use Facebook to recruit, you can post information about a job with a link to your organization's career page. If your business Facebook page has posts and information, you make it easier to attract candidates and employees and to keep them informed. Using your personal Facebook account, you can find friends and family with whom you have lost touch or who do not live near you, and you can stay connected by looking at their photographs and activities. You could be visiting the Kenilworth Park and Aquatic Gardens in Washington, DC, see the stunning water lilies, and share the lilies with others by clicking on the Facebook icon on your mobile phone and entering in the *"What's on your mind?"* field, *"At Kenilworth Park & Aquatic Gardens in Washington, DC; these are the most spectacular water lilies I have ever seen, take a look!"* You then tap the

camera icon, and when your mobile photographs pop up, tap the water lilies image and upload the photograph. In this case, you won't be able to "tag" the lilies, though, because the lilies aren't Facebook users. People you have friended will see the water lilies in their news feeds. If you have a Twitter account *and* a Facebook account, and you elect to have your Tweets with Twitter post to your Facebook page, you can have the same post appear on Twitter and Facebook with a single click.

Water Lilies, Kenilworth Park and Aquatic Gardens, Washington, DC, courtesy of Tam Mai-Ryan, Photographer

Why friend other Facebook users? For a personal Facebook page, you may want to limit your circle of Facebook "friends," particularly if you have a lot of very personal information and photographs. Also remember that your friends' posts will appear in your news feed or timeline, so the more friends you have, the more chance your news feed will get cluttered with a lot of posts, messages, photographs, and games that are of no interest to you. As with Twitter, you will want many "friends" if you are using your personal Facebook page for professional purposes. This will help you to keep as many people as possible informed about your products and services and to connect them to your organization's website, blogs, and Twitter and LinkedIn pages. Again, as with Twitter, you can post information about products, services, and dates and locations for business events, with a link to the organization's website for more information. While it is easy to build your network of friends for a personal Facebook page, Facebook does not offer the friending feature for business Facebook pages. If you post interesting, informative, entertaining, relevant, and timely posts, the people who visit your organization's Facebook page can "like" it and comment on or share your posts, which may get attention from others. As with any social media site, it takes time and work to maintain your organization's Facebook page content, because you will need to continually post interesting and current information and images.

 LinkedIn

What is LinkedIn? LinkedIn, pictured in the accompanying screenshot image, could be called the business version of Facebook. It is a social media site where people and businesses connect and share information, and it is growing by one new member every minute. Your LinkedIn profile represents your professional life and contains information about your education, employment experience, and skills. You can upload a single photograph with your profile; most people use a more formal photograph that is reflective of their professional image. Your organization's business LinkedIn page can showcase products and services, show who works with you, include a link to a webpage or blog, and potentially reach millions of professionals.

When you sign up and become a LinkedIn user, you can search for people you know—colleagues, classmates, people you've done business with, friends, and others—and connect. (*Please note that in our discussion of LinkedIn, we use the terms "contact," "link," and "connection" interchangeably.)* You can stay in touch with and updated on colleagues and friends as they change jobs, locations, and e-mail addresses. When you connect with someone using LinkedIn, you select a category that describes your relationship and which organization or institution you have in common.

Each time you connect with a new person on LinkedIn, you have the opportunity to expand your network by connecting with that new person's links. If you are looking to find out information about someone and you search on LinkedIn, it will show you if you have connections in common (second-tier connections) or if your connections and theirs have connections in common (third-tier connections). When you find someone on LinkedIn whom you want to connect with but don't know personally, you can send them an invitation to link.

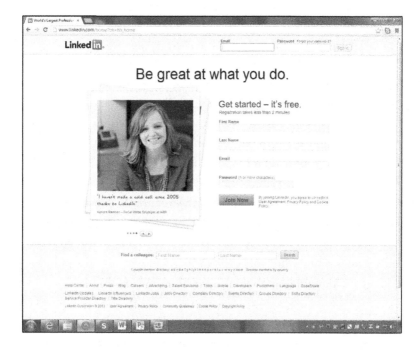

What are messages and InMail? You can send messages directly to the LinkedIn members you are connected to by clicking on their names. $$ If you subscribe and pay for the feature, you can send and receive messages to any LinkedIn member through a communication feature called InMail. Also, you can share thoughts, information, and updates with your entire LinkedIn network by sharing a general message from your home screen. Messages, InMail, and group communications are sent to the e-mail address that you have provide in your LinkedIn profile, making it easy for you to keep up.

Why join LinkedIn? If you are a business professional, being a member of LinkedIn will offer you many advantages—you will see that it is more than worth your effort if you leverage its capabilities. You can easily and quickly stay mutually updated on employment, education, and certification status with your business connections; send messages just to stay actively networked with some or all of your connections; keep your professional contact information updated in one place; send out requests for help with finding talent or information; and post information about job opportunities and service offerings. In addition, you can search for candidates with specific skills in specific geographic locations, send a request to communicate with candidates of interest, or if you have a common connection, ask for an introduction through your mutual link. *And,* if you have a meeting or are going on an interview with someone and you want to find out something about her background, you can demonstrate interest and initiative by searching for and reading about her on LinkedIn—and she can do the same about you. You have the opportunity to read recommendations for a candidate you are considering and learn more about the individual through querying the connections you have in common. All of this is to say that *if you are looking to hire talent, and you are not using LinkedIn, you are missing out.* If your organization establishes a LinkedIn page, its name is more likely to surface in Internet searches, thereby providing greater exposure to candidates, and you can use the LinkedIn Careers section to post job opportunities. $$ For an additional fee, you can subscribe to different levels of membership, which offer additional recruitment services.

Why connect with LinkedIn members? The larger your network within LinkedIn, the greater your reach will be when you use LinkedIn to find talent, look for opportunities yourself, stay connected with your network, and read and gather information. In LinkedIn, you can broaden your reach by joining groups that connect you to others beyond your one-to-one connections. You can ask questions; announce job openings; and publicize links, articles, and information. By building and growing your connections and groups, you will expand the universe of people who learn about you and your products, services, and job opportunities. If you share interesting, informative, entertaining, relevant, and timely posts, you will get more attention, interest, and referrals. As with any social media site, it takes time to build up and maintain a network. You will have a growing population of LinkedIn members with whom you can connect as people you know join LinkedIn and as your existing contacts make new connections. With LinkedIn, it is particularly advantageous to have as large a network as possible and to initiate as well as accept as many connections as you can to increase the audience for your candidate searches and to have a greater chance of being able to ask for an introduction to a candidate through the various tiers of your connections.

Below are just a couple of examples of established groups within LinkedIn that directly relate to the purpose of the handbook: social media recruiting.

- Recruiter The *Recruiter Network* is a recruiting and career networking social media group where you can network with recruiters; recruit talent; find a job or a headhunter; read recruiting, human resource, staffing, and employment news;

and make professional connections. The group has members in the US, UK, Europe, Canada, and India.

- *LinkedIn Jobs* is a career and networking group that has information about job openings, job leads, and job connections. The group has members in the US, UK, Europe, Canada, Asia, and India.

Google+

What is Google+? Google+ is Google's answer to social media, and you need to have a Google account to join. It is a newer social media site than the others discussed in this handbook, and while it is growing and becoming more known, it is still building a following. The Google+ initial offering was solely for personal pages, with no option for business pages. Google+ has some similarities to the look and feel of Facebook, but since it is a conceptual combination of several different social media sites, it has more functionality and flexibility. You can search by a topic and find a number of related communication threads and then select any of those threads and enter into a dialogue with people you don't know, simply by making a comment. You can upload single photographs with a posted message as well as create photograph albums with a whole series of photographs from specific events. Each photograph you upload can have a brief description, and the people in the photograph can be identified, or tagged. As with Facebook, you can find friends and family with whom you have lost touch or who do not live near you, and you can stay current and in touch by seeing photographs and posts. As you can see from the following bulleted explanations, with Google+ you can group your contacts into circles, get news feeds, engage in video chats, play games, do group messaging, and instantly upload your smartphone photographs.

- Circles: With circles, you can organize people in your Google+ connections into groups by category, such as friends, family, college mates, etc. From your circles page, you can drag and drop your connections into different circles, making it easy to tailor what you share with different people to their particular relationship with you. You can also put people in more than one circle. When you add someone to one of your circles for the first time, that person will receive notification but not the name(s) of the circle(s) in which you placed them. Like Facebook, there are privacy settings that allow you to manage who sees your photographs. Let's assume you have a circle named "College Mates" and another named "Family"; you could send information about a reunion to your College Mates circle and invite the people in your Family circle to a holiday celebration.

- Sparks: This is a news reader that brings news content to you automatically from your favorite websites. Each topic will get its own "Spark" page providing links to related articles, videos, and photographs.

- Hangouts: These are virtual rooms where you can video-chat with people in your circles. For example, you could start a hangout with people in one particular circle whom you would like to join you for a concert or sporting event you plan to attend.

- Huddles: This is group messaging for people within your circles. There's also a mobile app for smartphones that lets you send messages from your phone—you just select your group, and everyone can chat with each other.

- Instant uploads: When you take a photograph on your smartphone, it's automatically uploaded to a private album on Google+. You can then choose to share photographs to circles or just store photographs privately as a backup.

What are posts? Posts are messages you enter in Google+ on your stream. You can post any information you wish to share with others, like your thoughts or activities, and you can include photographs, videos, and links. Unlike Twitter, Google+ posts are not limited to 140 characters; like Facebook, comments to your posts appear beneath the original post, so that you have more of a dialogue. You can target your messages by designating messages as "public," so the messages can be seen by everyone on the web, or as "limited," which can only be shared with a selected circle or circles. If you use your personal Google+ page to recruit, you can post information about a job and include a link to your organization's career page.

Why join Google+? If you are a fan of Google products, Google+ may be a good social media option for you. While it is newer and has fewer users than Twitter, Facebook, or LinkedIn, it combines features of all three. Because of features like blogging, e-mail, chat, video, and news feeds, Google+ has the potential to become a dominant social media player. There certainly is no one social media site that can meet all your needs, but Google+ has made greater strides in that direction than Twitter, Facebook, and LinkedIn have.

Why connect with Google+ members? For the same reason we have discussed for the other social media sites: the larger your network, the greater your reach. You can broaden your reach easily by engaging in dialogue on topics of interest to you with people outside your circles so that others in the Google+ network with whom you would not ordinarily have any connection can learn about and connect with you. While it is still too soon to tell if Google+ will become a viable social media site for business, and thus for recruiting, you can still have a personal account and use it to recruit for your organization by announcing jobs and searching for members who might be potential candidates.

Are you ready to go to the next step and actually set up social media sites?

First, find out how much you have retained ...

> 1. Twitter limits the length of posts to _____ characters.
> 2. True or false: InMail is the basic feature by which LinkedIn users communicate with each other.
> 3. Of the four social media sites discussed in this handbook, the one that offers the most features is:
>   a. LinkedIn.
>   b. Twitter.
>   c. Google+.
>   d. Facebook.

> Answers: 1. 140; 2. false; 3. c

Congratulations! You now have a basic grasp of the key social media sites. Now let's move on to the heart of the matter—actually joining the four social media sites we have reviewed in this section.

How to Create Your Social Media Sites

Step-by-step instructions for setting up Twitter, Facebook, LinkedIn, and Google+

In this section, we will discuss how to join and benefit from four widely used social media sites, each of which can be enormously effective in helping you recruit: Twitter, Facebook, LinkedIn, and Google+. The focus of this section is the business use of these social media sites, but you can apply this to your personal use as well. We suggest that you select and focus on one or two social media sites to start and then expand into using the others as you become more familiar with the features and functionality of social media in general.

Once you set up these social media pages for your organization, you can incorporate the tools and applications that will make the most of your social media communication efforts. *We'll address this topic fully in the section called "Tools and Tips to Maximize Your Use of Social Media," so if your organization already has a presence on Twitter, Facebook, LinkedIn, and Google+, you can skip directly to that section.* Please note that the tools and sources we name in this handbook are representative examples of the many ways to use social media for recruiting. They are provided for your reference, but hyrebuzz does not guarantee any one particular tool or resource. Before getting started, you should research the various options available and select those that best fit your needs.

Of course, the Internet is never without a certain risk to privacy. We'll remind you of the following cautions in the step-by-step instructions, but we want to highlight the cautions before we begin.

‼ Cautions:

- Exercise discretion about uploading your entire contacts file. Most social media sites will give you the option to upload your contacts, but we recommend that—in order to protect the privacy of your friends and family—you wait to do this until you have become a skilled user of social media sites.

- Log out of your personal social media accounts before building or working in business social media accounts to prevent the accounts from being linked.

- Choose the username for the social media account profile and e-mail address of your social media administrator carefully, as it ties to business social media sites for administration and communication purposes. Your organization must be able to terminate an employee's access immediately, at any time, as necessary to protect the integrity of its social media accounts.

Not using social media? If you are not already using social media, you may want to first set up personal pages on these sites to increase your comfort level and understanding of what the sites have to offer. This will increase your success in selling the use of social media as part of your employer's recruitment strategy. As you use social media sites for your personal networking, you'll quickly begin to understand their utility and the positive impact the sites can have on your recruiting efforts. Your personal experience with the sites will also lay the groundwork for you to establish a social media strategy for your employer, a critical step we will discuss in detail in its own section later in this handbook.

Let's get started! Use the following checklist to gather the basics of what you need to get started setting up social media sites.

Checklist: What You Need Before You Begin Setting Up Social Media Accounts	Notes and Progress Log
☐ **<u>Strategy and Policy/Guidelines</u>** *Develop a social media strategy and policy/guidelines, which will establish the guidelines for use and maintenance of your organization's social media pages. We will discuss this concept in detail in the section titled "Strategy and Policy/Guidelines."* ☐ Establish a clear purpose that your pages will serve, such as marketing, sales, name branding, image, publicity, communication, recruitment, and creating a competitive edge. ☐ Determine what types of posts will support the purpose of your various social media accounts, what information will interest and build followers, and how much variety to build into your posts. ☐ Keep in mind that it is important to post current and forward-thinking information of interest to the type of followers you want to attract; if you only post about what you want from your followers, you won't keep those followers. ☐ Identify who has responsibility and authority for posting, maintenance, and deciding which organizations and individuals your organization wants to connect with (follow, friend, link) through social media sites; this will be clear once you establish your strategy and policy/guidelines. *See "Posting and Maintenance" in the next checklist for more details.* ☐ Set guidelines for employee use of social media sites. *See the section entitled "Strategy and Policy/Guidelines."*	

Checklist: What You Need Before You Begin Setting Up Social Media Accounts	Notes and Progress Log
☐ **Posting and Maintenance** *In order to create a well-maintained and cohesive social media presence, it is important to establish:* ☐ Who will create and approve content, photographs, digital images, and videos. ☐ The person whose social media page(s) and/or personal information and e-mail address will be used to set up your organization's social media site(s). ❗❗ When making this decision, consider the character of the person you select. He or she will receive and respond to e-mail notifications and postings on behalf of the organization, and the organization must be able to terminate the social media administrator's access immediately, at any time, as necessary to protect the integrity of its social media accounts without disrupting account operations. For this reason, consider using a fictitious name or contracting with a vendor. ☐ How often and when to post based upon your audience—understand how your audience uses social media; for example, since adults use social media most during evenings and weekends and at the beginning, middle, and end of the workday, you may want to post job announcements in the morning. ☐ Who will monitor sites and coordinate, change, and remove postings throughout the day and week. ☐ Who will ensure that the site conveys what your organization wants it to convey.	

Checklist: What You Need Before You Begin Setting Up Social Media Accounts	Notes and Progress Log
☐ **IT Support** ☐ Enlist the help of your organization's web or information technologists to develop your social media strategy and set up your social media pages; if you do not have this kind of support, identify a friend, relative, or colleague who knows social media and can answer questions for you.	

☐ **Address**
    ☐ Select a unique address or username for each social media site (note that Facebook allows duplication of names). It should be unique enough to be available and usable across all of the sites you wish to use. You can check the availability of your organization's name on each site by Google-searching your organization's address as it would appear for each social media site. For example, at hyrebuzz we searched as follows: *"@hyrebuzz"* for Twitter, *"hyrebuzz@facebook"* for Facebook, *"hyrebuzz@linkedin.com"* for LinkedIn, and *"hyrebuzz@gmail.com"* for Google+.
    ☐ Log in to Twitter, Facebook, LinkedIn, and Google+ and see if the address/name you want to use is available; if not, decide on an available name that is similar enough to reflect your organization's identity. For example, when hyrebuzz cofounder Kathy Mulder-Williamson was developing a website and social media pages for her recruiting company, Recruiter Dynamics, LLC, the name @RecruiterDynamics was too long for Twitter, so she used @Recruitdynamics,	

Checklist: What You Need Before You Begin Setting Up Social Media Accounts	Notes and Progress Log
since there is a strong resemblance between the two. Even if you don't want to fully launch numerous social media sites, reserve a name for the key sites so that it will be available to you in the future. ☐ Use a domain name vendor like Network Solutions to check the availability of domain names for your organization if your organization does not already have a website.	
☐ **Profile Picture or Avatar** ☐ Select the image you will be using to identify your organization on social media sites, and get a digital file of that image so that you can upload it to the various social media sites. The size of profile pictures varies on each social media page, as shown below, and you must size your profile picture or avatar to fit before uploading it. You can use free image-sizing tools such as www.irfanview.com to size your profile picture or avatar according to the size requirements for each site. You may want to check whether these sizes have changed. **Twitter:** No more than 128 x 128 pixels or 48 x 48 thumbnails **Facebook:** 180 x 180 pixels **LinkedIn:** 200 x 200 pixels; use .jpg, .gif, or .png file **Google+:** 250 x 250 pixels	

Checklist: What You Need Before You Begin Setting Up Social Media Accounts	Notes and Progress Log

☐ **<u>Bio, Products, and Services</u>**
    ☐ Visit the social media pages of your competitive community to see how they present themselves and how the content and profile pictures or avatars vary by site.
    ☐ Decide what content and images you want to appear on your organization's various social media pages.
    ☐ Prepare content and images to upload to each site; these will vary, because each site is different. For example, for Twitter you must write a very brief bio, while on LinkedIn there are overview and services tabs where you can present quite a bit of information about your organization and its offerings.	

☐ **<u>Website</u>**
If your organization does not have a website, you can still use social media to recruit; some sites may require at least a registered URL.
    ☐ Download icons from Google images for each of your social media pages to place on your organization's website.
    ☐ Coordinate with your web or information technologist to ensure that those icons are placed prominently and link to the appropriate social media page.
    ☐ Consider creating a website for your organization if it does not have one. **$$** While a sophisticated, attractive website with a high degree of functionality is costly, you can create a basic website somewhat inexpensively. *For tips on building a cost-effective website, see the section entitled "Tools and Tips to Maximize Your Use of Social Media."*	

Checklist: What You Need Before You Begin Setting Up Social Media Accounts	Notes and Progress Log
☐ **Applicant Tracking Systems*** ☐ Ensure that your applicant tracking system is linked to the careers page on your organization's website. ☐ Contact your applicant tracking system vendor and discuss how to connect it with social media. **NOTE: If your organization does not have an applicant tracking system, you can still use social media to recruit; however, if you would like to get one, see the section called "Applicant Tracking System—Why it is important to use in conjunction with social media" for suggestions.*	

Now are you ready to set up your organization's Twitter page?

This will be fun and simple! If you are prepared in advance, you won't need more than an hour to set up all four social media pages. We will walk you through setting up your organization's Twitter, Facebook, LinkedIn, and Google+ pages and provide you with useful tips that will help you to save time and make the most of your social media pages specifically when recruiting.

Start by going to www.twitter.com, and you will see a screenshot like the accompanying image. Then work down the checklist that follows to set up your Twitter page. The key to successfully using Twitter is to gain followers by using hashtags strategically so that your Tweets with Twitter have an audience. Building a following can be time consuming. Twitter users typically follow friends, relatives, and famous people they admire and are interested in or who have a reputation for posting interesting Tweets with Twitter. Depending on how well known your organization is or how creative your Tweets with Twitter are, you might have to do some coaxing to get people to follow you.

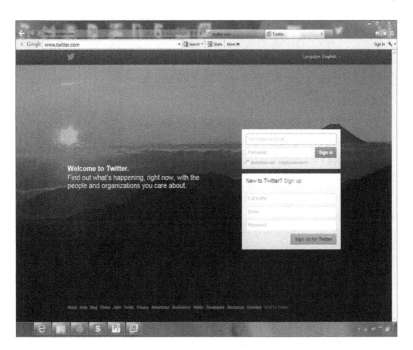

Steps for Setting Up Your Organization's Twitter Page	Notes and Progress Log
☐ **Profile** *Read this entire checklist and visit the Twitter pages of your competitive community before you enter any information. Make notes to the right for easy reference as you get to each step.* ☐ Be sure that your personal Twitter account isn't open while you are setting up your organization's Twitter account. ☐ Enter your organization's full name in the field "New to Twitter? Join Today!" (You'll already have selected your organization's Twitter username from following the address search instructions in the "Before You Begin" checklist above.)	

Steps for Setting Up Your Organization's Twitter Page	Notes and Progress Log
☐ Enter the e-mail address of your organization's Twitter page administrator.	
☐ ‼ Create and enter a high-security password that cannot be easily hacked. Hackers are *very* active on Twitter.	
☐ Click the gold "Sign Up" button, and you will be taken to the setup "Join Twitter" page.	
☐ Review the information you have entered and make any changes.	
☐ Click on the "Create my account" button, and you will be taken to the "Welcome" page, where you will be greeted by "The Twitter Teacher," who introduces you to Twitter.	
☐ Click on the "Next" button, and you will be taken to "Build your timeline," where you can practice following. For your first follow, enter *"@hyrebuzz"* in the search box at the top of the page, click on the search icon, and when hyrebuzz appears, click on the "Follow" button, which will turn into the "Following" button, confirming your follow.	
☐ Practice a second follow by entering *"@Recruitdynamics"* in the search box at the top of the page and clicking on the search icon. When Recruiter Dynamics appears, repeat the steps you did for hyrebuzz above.	
☐ Practice more follows, and when you are done, click on the "Next" button at the top of the page.	

Steps for Setting Up Your Organization's Twitter Page	Notes and Progress Log
☐ **‼** We recommend that you skip the "Find people you know" practice page when setting up a business Twitter profile because this feature will search the contact list of the e-mail address associated with the account. Depending on what you use this e-mail address for, it may contain personal contacts. Click on "Skip this step" at the bottom right (this location may change).	
☐ Upload a photograph or avatar before Tweeting so that your account is complete and followers can recognize you by sight. Under "Add character," click on "Upload image." Upload the image you have selected to represent your organization on Twitter by navigating to its location on your computer or network and selecting the digital profile picture or avatar to upload. Remember to size this to 128 x 128 pixels or less, or 48 x 48 thumbnails, before uploading it (you may want to check to see that these sizes have not changed).	
☐ Assess whether the uploaded profile picture or avatar works in Twitter format, and if not, resize the profile picture or avatar or find one that works better. The profile picture or avatar will appear compressed to a very small size to the left of all of your Tweets with Twitter. *Since it may be difficult to see, you may have to try a number of different images until you find one that best represents your organization.*	

Steps for Setting Up Your Organization's Twitter Page	Notes and Progress Log
☐ Complete the bio section by entering the blurb you have created for your organization. With a 160-character limit, you must be succinct but descriptive enough that followers can easily understand your organization's mission, products, and services. Click "Done" and—ta da!—you will see your Twitter page.	
☐ You'll find an e-mail from Twitter in your e-mail inbox. Click the link in the e-mail to confirm your e-mail address.	
☐ Return to Twitter and click on the hyperlink to your Twitter account name above "View my profile page" at the top left of the page (this location may change).	
☐ Next, click on the sprocket wheel drop-down box on the top right of the page, to the left of the blue "Compose new Tweet" icon, choose "Settings," then "Profile" (this location may change), and enter your organization's name, location, and website URL. If you are ready to add Twitter to your organization's website, click "You can also add Twitter to your site here" and follow the instructions.	
☐ Wait to click the "Post your Tweets to Facebook" button until you have a Facebook page set up.	
☐ Click the blue "Save changes" button when you are finished, and then click "Home" located in the navigation bar along the top of the page to go to your main Twitter page and view what you have set up.	

Steps for Setting Up Your Organization's Twitter Page	Notes and Progress Log
☐ Use hyrebuzz to try a test Tweet with Twitter. Click in the field called "Compose new Tweet ..." at the top left of your Twitter page (this location may change), enter your message *("@hyrebuzz this is a test Tweet")*, and click on the "Tweet" button beneath that box (this location may change), and your Tweet with Twitter will post. ☐ Refer to the Tools and Tips section for information on following Twitter users and getting Twitter followers.	

Whew, you're done with Twitter! Now let's move on to setting up your organization's Facebook page.

Go to www.facebook.com and follow the steps in the checklist to set up your Facebook page. Check off each step when complete, and make notes to the right. The key to successfully using Facebook is expanding your list of people who "like" you (if you are using a business page) or who are your "friends" (if you are using a personal page). The more people you are connected to, the more candidates, employees, contractors, vendors, affiliates, members, customers, partners, residents, and benefactors will see your information. Facebook differentiates between business and personal pages; for example, on your business Facebook page you will build a fan base or audience, while on your personal Facebook page, you will build friends.

‼ Keep in mind when building your business Facebook network that users commonly use Facebook for personal connections and relatives. In addition, Facebook requires an individual's name, e-mail address, and date of birth in order to set up a page, so your organization's

Facebook page will be tied to someone in the organization. This means that when he or she leaves, you may need to change the e-mail address associated with the page or the Facebook user designated as an administrator so the originator can no longer log in to your organization's Facebook page as an administrator. This highlights the importance of giving serious thought to the individual who is designated as the page administrator.

Steps for Setting Up Your Organization's Facebook Page	Notes and Progress Log
☐ **Profile** *Read this entire checklist and visit the Facebook pages of your competitive community before you enter any information. Make notes to the right for easy reference as you get to each step.* ☐ Be sure that your personal Facebook account is not open while you are setting up your organization's Facebook account, unless you want your personal account to be associated with your organization's business account. ☐ Click "Create a Page for a celebrity, band, or business." You will find this under the green "Sign Up" button on the right below the fields where individuals enter their information (this location may change). ☐ Select the option that best describes your organization (local business or place; company, organization, or institution; brand or product; artist, band, or public figure; entertainment; cause or community). ☐ Choose the category that best describes your organization from the drop-down box.	

Steps for Setting Up Your Organization's Facebook Page	Notes and Progress Log
☐ Enter the name of your organization, agree to the terms, and click on "Get Started."	
☐ Enter the e-mail address to which Facebook e-mail notifications will be sent. This helps to separate your personal Facebook account from your organization's. (We recommend that this e-mail address not be associated with any personal social media accounts.)	
☐ Select and enter a password.	
☐ Enter a date of birth (this is still a requirement, even for a professional Facebook page).	
☐ Complete the "Security Check" and agree to the terms.	
☐ Click on the blue "Sign Up Now!" button.	
☐ Confirm your e-mail address by clicking on the confirmation link in the e-mail that Facebook will send to your e-mail inbox.	
☐ Upload an image for your organization's profile picture or avatar. This will likely be the official logo. Remember to size the file to 180 x 180 pixels before uploading it (you may want to check to see if these sizes have changed).	
☐ Enter in a description of your organization that is less than 255 words long, add the URL for your organization's website, and click "Save Info."	
☐ Click "Skip" in the bottom right-hand corner (this location may change) at the "Enable Ads" step (**\$\$** you may elect to enable ads, but you must pay extra for this service).	

Steps for Setting Up Your Organization's Facebook Page	Notes and Progress Log
☐ Click on "Edit Page," choose "Manage Notifications" from the drop-down menu, and indicate whether you want notifications sent to your e-mail address when people post or make a comment, and save changes by clicking the blue button at the bottom of the page when you are done.	
☐ Choose "Manage Permissions" from the "Edit Page" drop-down menu; enter your selections for restrictions, posting, and block-listing; and save changes when you are done. To find more information on these options in Facebook, click on the "What's this?" link.	
☐ Click "Basic Information" on the left-hand side of the screen (this location may change) and enter detailed information about your organization, such as the year it was founded, its address, and its mission. Always save changes when you are done.	
☐ Click on "Resources" and read more about expanded tools and best practices for developing your Facebook page and connecting with people.	
☐ Build a fan base or audience for your business Facebook page by sending a broadcast e-mail with an embedded Facebook page hyperlink to employees, contractors, vendors, affiliates, members, partners, residents, benefactors, and customers to ask them to become a fan and "like" you.	
☐ **"Like" hyrebuzz on Facebook, let us know how you found us, and give us a status report.**	

Steps for Setting Up Your Organization's Facebook Page	Notes and Progress Log
☐ Log in to your business Twitter page and elect to "Post your Tweets to Facebook." ☐ Post job openings, engaging content, photos, videos, and questions on your admin panel under "Status."	

Hey, you're halfway there! Are you ready to set up a LinkedIn page?

Go to www.linkedin.com, which looks like the accompanying screenshot. Follow the steps in the checklist to set up your LinkedIn page, check off each step when complete, and make notes to the right. The key to successfully using LinkedIn is to connect with as many people (clients, members, employees, contractors, vendors, committees, affiliates, partners, residents, benefactors) as possible. Expanding your LinkedIn network is easy, because once you connect to one person, you have the opportunity to connect with their network. Note that the LinkedIn page for your organization must be associated with the LinkedIn page of an individual, and that individual must first set up his or her own LinkedIn page.

Steps for Setting Up Your Organization's LinkedIn Page	Notes and Progress Log
☐ **Personal Profile** *Before you can set up an organization profile, you must set up the personal profile of the individual (this can be a fictitious user) whose LinkedIn page will be connected to your organization's page and who will serve as the page administrator. Skip to the Organization Profile checklist if you already have a personal LinkedIn page or if you have established a fictitious user who will be connected to your organization's LinkedIn page.* ☐ Enter the user's first and last names, e-mail address, and password under "Get started—it's free" and click "Join Now." ☐ Enter the user's country, zip code, employment status, job title, company name, and industry. ☐ Click "Create my profile," and the next screen will ask you to enter an e-mail address and password to search your existing contact list to find people you already know in LinkedIn. ☐ ‼ *We recommend that you leave these fields blank until you become more familiar with LinkedIn. Just click "Skip this step," located beneath the dialogue box (this location may change).* ☐ Check your e-mail for an e-mail message from LinkedIn. ☐ ‼ Confirm your e-mail address by clicking on the URL below and not on the "Click Here" hyperlink.	

Steps for Setting Up Your Organization's LinkedIn Page	Notes and Progress Log
☐ **!!** Click on *"Skip this step"* on the welcome screen when you are asked to enter your e-mail address and password, as it will provide LinkedIn with access to your personal address book.	
☐ Click on "Continue."	
☐ Elect to "share" by clicking on the Twitter and Facebook icons if you want to share postings between these three social media sites.	
☐ Authorize LinkedIn to use your account to connect to Twitter and Facebook, and you will be directed to enter your Twitter and Facebook login and password information.	
☐ **$$** Choose your plan level once the LinkedIn account is set up; some plan levels are free. *NOTE: We recommend that you elect the Basic Plan until you are familiar with LinkedIn, understand its value, and take LinkedIn training (you can sign up for free training on LinkedIn).*	
☐ Complete your profile by entering information about your start dates, employment, education, interests, groups, associations, honors, and awards—and also your personal information.	
☐ Click on the "Finished" button when you have entered all of your information.	

Steps for Setting Up Your Organization's LinkedIn Page	Notes and Progress Log
☐ **<u>Organization Profile</u>**	
☐ Be sure that your personal LinkedIn account is not open while you are setting up your organization's LinkedIn account, unless you will be administering the organization account from your personal account.	
☐ Go to your LinkedIn home screen, hover over the "Companies" tab, select "Find Companies" from the drop-down menu, and click on "Add a Company," which is located to the right (this location may change).	
☐ Enter your organization's name under "Company name" and the e-mail address under "Your e-mail address at company"; click on the check box to verify that you are an official representative of your organization, and click "Continue."	
☐ Check the e-mail for the LinkedIn approval to establish a new business account, and follow the e-mail instructions for reconfirming the e-mail address. If you receive a red error message at this point, you will not be able to continue creating the account, and you will need to e-mail LinkedIn for assistance. If you did not receive this message, move to the next step.	
☐ Sign in to LinkedIn again and begin building your organization's LinkedIn page.	
☐ Answer administrative questions in the "Overview" tab to designate languages, page administration, users, status updates, company type, industry, operating status, year founded, and locations.	

Steps for Setting Up Your Organization's LinkedIn Page	Notes and Progress Log
☐ Upload your organization's logo. Remember to size the logo to a minimum of 200 x 200 pixels and to use a .jpg, .gif, or .png file before uploading it (you may want to check to see if these sizes have changed).	
☐ Enter in the "Company Description" field general information that describes your organization, such as what appears on your website's home or "about us" page or your mission, products, services, and history. *NOTE: This will be the first thing visitors will see, so make it a friendly and/or creative introduction to your organization and its products and services.*	
☐ Identify as many core competencies as your organization has, and include them in the "Company Specialties" section so that LinkedIn members searching by topic will be drawn to your organization's profile.	
☐ Save your entries on the "Overview" page by clicking on "Publish" at the top of the page when you are finished.	
☐ $$ Skip over the "Careers" page until such time as you are ready to post and pay for job-opening announcements.	
☐ Go to the "Products & Services" tab and click on "Add a product & service."	
☐ Provide information regarding products, services, features, disclaimers, promotions, category, contacts, and video; if desired, upload a product/service-related image. Create a page that is interesting and informative and be sure to ask for recommendations so	

Steps for Setting Up Your Organization's LinkedIn Page	Notes and Progress Log
that visitors to the page can see connections you have in common and be impressed by what your clients, members, and vendors have to say.	
☐ Save your entries on the "Products & Services" page by clicking on "Publish" at the top of the page when you are finished.	
☐ Click on the "Analytics" tab to familiarize yourself with what types of information are tracked and presented regarding your organization's LinkedIn page followers, visitors, and views; this information is visible only to you or your company page administrator.	
☐ Check Analytics regularly to help you understand your followers, what those followers do, and who else they follow; to determine if you are getting what you want from your organization's LinkedIn page; and to help you strategize.	
☐ Post status updates for your organization regarding new products and services, promotions, news, and articles to get LinkedIn followers and members updated, interested, and posting comments and likes.	
☐ **Find hyrebuzz on LinkedIn, link with us, and let us know you have progressed to this point in our handbook!**	

Time to wrap it up—are you ready to tackle the last social media site on our list, Google+?

As with other social media sites, your organization's Google+ account must be associated with an individual's Google account, so your social media administrator must have a Google account in order to set up a Google+ account. A free Google account includes access to many Google web-user services, like e-mail (called Gmail), document storage, and a calendar; the most familiar of these is probably Gmail, and in fact many people use the terms "Google account" and "Gmail account" interchangeably. So, in order to get started setting up your organization's Google+ account, identify whose Google account/Gmail address will be used. You may wish to have a fictitious user as explained earlier. Once the Google account is ready (you can follow the steps below to create it), go to www.google.com/+/business, and you will see a screen like the accompanying screenshot. Next, follow the steps in the checklist, check off each step you complete, and make any notes to the right.

The key to successfully using Google+ is to get people to add you to their circles, so include ways to gain connections in your social media strategy and decide what circles to establish. You can't add people to your organization's Google+ circles unless your organization is in a circle of theirs, so invite those whom you want to be involved in your organization's Google+ circles.

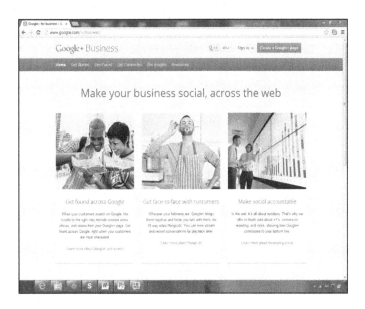

Steps for Setting Up Your Organization's Google+ Account	Notes and Progress Log
☐ **Personal Profile** *Skip this step if the personal Google account that will be connected to your organization's Google+ account has already been established.* ☐ Create a Google account by going to accounts.google.com and clicking on the "create an account for free" hyperlink on the upper left-hand side of the page (this location may change). ☐ Enter first name and last name, choose a username, create and confirm a password, and enter a birthday, gender, and mobile phone. ☐ *NOTE: From now on, when you want to work with your organization's Google+ page, you will sign in to this personal Google account; then in the bar at the top of the screen, you'll see a link on the far left with a plus sign beside your name (e.g., "+Patrick") (these locations may change).* ☐ *Click there, and it will take you to the designated administrator's Google+ page. Once your associated organization page is set up, you can click on the profile picture in the top right corner (this location may change) of the administrator's personal Google+ page; a drop-down menu will appear, allowing you to select whether you want to work with the administrator's personal Google+ page or the organization's Google+ page.*	

Steps for Setting Up Your Organization's Google+ Account	Notes and Progress Log

☐ **Organization Profile**
   ☐ Go to www.google.com/+/business and click on "Create your Google+ page" on the top left corner of the page (this location may change).
   ☐ Be sure that you are signed in to the Google account that you want to use to administer your organization's Google+ page.
   ☐ Choose from "Pick category" the category that describes your organization, and enter the name of your organization and the URL of its website (optional).
   ☐ Select the appropriate demographic group from the drop-down box, check the box to agree to the terms, and click on "Continue."
   ☐ "Get Started," make your page come alive, and upload photographs and logos that will represent your organization. Ensure that you have sized any photos to 250 x 250 pixels (you may want to check to see if these sizes have changed).
   ☐ Enter a brief tagline under "Describe this page." We recommend that this be consistent with your organization's website and other social media pages.
   ☐ Select from the options in the "How can people contact this page?" drop-down box.
   ☐ Click on "Finish" and you will receive a message congratulating you on your new Google+ page.	

Steps for Setting Up Your Organization's Google+ Account	Notes and Progress Log
☐ Click on "Settings" located on the bottom right of the page (this location may change) and verify that the selections are appropriate for your organization's Google+ page.	
☐ Click on "Get Started" located on the bottom right of the page (this location may change) to learn more about the functionality and advanced tools of Google+.	
☐ Click "Circles" in the far left column (this location may change) and name circles based on how you want to separate your communications (you can create separate circles like clients, members, employees, contractors, vendors, committees, affiliates, partners, residents, benefactors, etc.). Your contacts won't know the name of the circle you put them in, so don't worry about offending anyone.	
☐ Complete the page—upload pictures, upload videos, populate your circles, create a link to your organization's website, put in custom links (e.g., Twitter, Facebook, LinkedIn), and add contact information.	
☐ Start using Google+; post a message or job opportunity.	
☐ Invite people to add *you* to *their* circles so that you can add them to your circles, because you can't add people to your organization's Google+ circles unless your organization is in one of their circles.	
☐ **Add hyrebuzz to one of your circles and let us know how you are progressing with your setup and use of social media.**	

You know what time it is! Quiz yourself on your progress ...

1. A Twitter bio can be up to ____ characters in length.
2. True or false: You must have an applicant tracking system to use social media for recruiting.
3. This handbook recommends that your business Facebook page connect with:
    a. Friends.
    b. Fans.
    c. Circles.

Answers: 1. 160; 2. false; 3. b

Get it done easier, faster, and more efficiently

Y ou've got accounts set up on the four most common social media sites. Now what? You know how to use social media; now how do you maximize its utility when it comes to recruiting? In this section, we list some tools and tips that can shortcut the process and optimize your online recruiting.

AddThis. AddThis and similar tools help you to integrate social media directly into your organization's website. AddThis embeds a social media icon into your website; visitors simply click on the icon to quickly navigate to your various social media pages. This particular tool also provides analytics, so you can track the volume and popularity of your social media pages.

Applicant Tracking Systems (ATS). Some ATSs take on the job of spreading the word for you by allowing you to post a job once to your ATS and then automatically broadcasting that job announcement to your social media sites as well as numerous other job boards. If you take advantage of this capability, it will streamline your job-posting efforts and get your posting out to multiple sites instantaneously. But that's just the beginning. We have devoted an entire section to ATSs, so please refer to that for a more comprehensive discussion.

Bar codes. When you embed a bar code into your job posting, a candidate can link directly to your website by taking a picture of the bar code using a QR code app on his or her smartphone. This tool is particularly effective at job fairs and on posted signs.

Blogs. We recommend that you incorporate blogging into your recruitment strategy. Many blogs are free and easy to set up. You can increase your chances of getting hits when candidates do searches by blogging about your organization and its opportunities and embedding the blog link into your organization's website and social media pages. Popular blog sites include wordpress.com, blogger.com, and pimpmyblog.com.

Create a talent network. Why not take your organization's careers page to another level? Add a sense of your organization's unique identity by including attractive and interesting features like videos, testimonials, blogs, and groups. This extra dose of originality will help create a flow of active visitors to your careers page who come for more than a passing glance at your current opportunities. Not only will this help to brand, create buzz, and make your organization an employer of choice, but it will also build a broader network of contacts with whom you can actively communicate—not just about job opportunities, but also about future developments in your organization, products and services, growth and change, and marketing information. You might also want to explore using job boards that have network-building features.

Facebook career network. Facebook has an app called "BranchOut," which allows users to easily network within their social graph (a "social graph" is an online network as opposed to a real-world network). **$$** While the app is free to users and recruiters, there is a fee for posting job opportunities.

Free postings and searches. Free sites like jobspider.com, postjobsfree.com, and findajobalready.com allow employers and candidates to post and search for résumés or curricula vitae and jobs.

We don't endorse any of these in particular but want you to be aware of their existence should you want to give the sites a try.

Intern job board. **$$** Organizations can pay to post internship opportunities on a website called InternMatch, which students seeking internships can search for free.

Job-posting aggregators. Postjobsforfree, Ziprecruiter, and Bullhorn are a few of the aggregators, or one-stop shops, where you can post jobs on multiple boards. You use these tools to post a job once, and the aggregators broadcast your notice to numerous other job boards and social media sites. By using these aggregators, you save time and accelerate the dissemination of your opportunities. These aggregators also come with an added bonus: many other sites to which the aggregators might not broadcast automatically pick up their postings.

Join user groups to market your organization. You can market your organization by joining user groups within your industry and in the general cloud community on sites like Yahoo, Google, and LinkedIn.

LinkedIn follows. Follow companies on LinkedIn by searching by name and then hovering over their LinkedIn profile and clicking "Follow Company."

Mention. A mention is any Twitter update that contains "@username" anywhere in the body of the Tweet with Twitter; this includes @replies.

Mobile technology. Mobile media, communications, and technology—such as text messaging—are emerging tools for recruiting that will soon become a standard part of the recruitment communications you utilize to attract and engage prospective talent.

PDF conversion. To help you download and convert résumés from one format to another, there are free tools, such as Nitro PDF Professional, that will convert a document from MSWord to PDF and vice versa.

Remote document access. If you don't have tools that allow you remote access to your stored résumés or curriculum vitae and other working papers, check out tools such as Dropbox and ResumeBucket. These tools enable you to store and retrieve documents, photographs, and videos online (or "in the cloud") from any computer, smartphone, or tablet by logging in to an account you establish.

RSS feeds. An RSS (rich site summary, also called really simple syndication) feed delivers regularly changing web content to you, allowing you to keep track of what's going on with numerous websites without having to take the time to visit them all separately. If you want to embed an RSS feed, enlist the help of your IT administrator or use an RSS feed tool to help you, such as www.rssinclude.com. By subscribing to RSS feeds that are appropriate to your industry and interests, such as RSS feeds from recruiterblog.com, you will get updated information on hot topics related to staffing and recruitment technologies. In addition, you can embed RSS feeds on a website or social media site and pull current, interesting information from other websites to appeal to and draw in an audience—be it employees, contractors, vendors, affiliates, partners, members, customers, residents, and benefactors. For an example, visit www.recruiterdynamics.com and see the RSS feeds at the bottom left of the home page, which display rolling blog job postings and broadcasts from SHRM Online (the website of the Society for Human Resource Management). These RSS feeds to the Recruiter Dynamics website provide informative professional information to visitors.

Schedule Tweets. So that you don't have to log in to Twitter constantly to post Tweets with Twitter, you can use tools to preschedule Tweets with Twitter to be released later. This means that you can post days worth of Tweets with Twitter at one time! There are numerous tools available. **$$** Since the tools vary in the features offered and some charge a fee, here are several options so that you can search for the one that best suits your organization's need: cotweet.com, taweet.com, twuffer.com, futuretweets.com, tweetdeck.com.

Search for specific candidates. When you are given the name of a potential candidate but have no contact information, you can use tools like Spoke and Anywho to help you find them.

Shorten Tweets. Since Tweets with Twitter are limited to 140 characters, it can be a challenge to Tweet with Twitter enough content about a job and still include a link to your website's careers page or applicant tracking system. Tools like bitly, at bitly.com (see accompanying screenshot), shorten links. Just paste in the URL and click the "Shorten" button; then copy and paste the compressed link into Twitter.

Size profile pictures or avatars. As each social networking site has different sizing, tools like Irfanview will resize your profile picture or avatar to the appropriate dimensions.

Social media management tools. **$$** There are a number of tools that help you manage and coordinate your social media account use and results, including TweetDeck, CoTweet, HootSuite, Involver, and SproutSocial. TweetDeck is free; the others are not. Social media management tools can reduce the amount of time you spend by allowing you to use and track multiple social media sites through a single tool. You can accomplish things like scheduling Tweets with Twitter for later posting; posting messages on multiple accounts and social media sites with one post; managing multiple Twitter accounts; tracking your social media results; using social analytics; monitoring your mentions; using a mobile app for communicating on the go; filtering unwanted updates to your account; and viewing in multiple columns at one time your search results, favorites, mentions, and hashtag references.

Text messaging. Text messaging candidates is a faster and more effective way to reach candidates than e-mail and voice mail. If you text a large number of candidates, a mobile app can help you track incoming messages.

Twitter.

> **Communication tips**. Writing engaging Tweets with Twitter that will build a following for your organization is key, but it's tough to do right. To help you Tweet with Twitter effectively, here are some tips that we have learned to maximize the impact of 140 characters.
>
> - To build and keep a following, focus Tweet topics on your followers, not on your organization.

- Develop a consistent style to your Tweets with Twitter so that followers come to know what to expect from the Tweets with Twitter.

- Tweet with Twitter articles, photographs, links to blogs and videos about your organization, job opportunities, Twitter tools, current events, and professional development.

- Tweet with Twitter special offers, discounts, and contests to entice new and retain current followers.

- Tweet with Twitter pictures! Pictures get heavily retweeted and spread around. There was a photograph of US Airways Flight 1549 floating in the Hudson that was viewed more than 350,000 times!

- Be brief, abbreviate words, and substitute words with digits— instead of "four" use "4."

- Schedule times of day and days of the week to Tweet with Twitter. Remember that adults Tweet with Twitter the most in either the morning, midday, or early evening. Start with one to three Tweets with Twitter per day, and do not Tweet with Twitter too much, or you will lose followers.

- Rotate Tweet with Twitter topics to keep followers interested. Let's say you are Tweeting with Twitter three times per day for two days:

    1. Day One. Tweet with Twitter about a helpful Twitter tool with a link to its website, an informative study with a link, and a job opportunity with a link to where to apply.

    2. Day Two. Tweet with Twitter about an industry-related

video with a YouTube link, ask an open-ended question about the study you Tweeted with Twitter the day before, and retweet a compelling Tweet with Twitter from someone who is high profile (we'll tell you how to retweet below).

- Acknowledge people whose Tweets with Twitter you see and like, whether or not they are following you—it's a great way to attract new followers by letting people know you're out there and to develop relationships with your existing followers.

- Use hashtags in Tweets with Twitter so that people who aren't following you might find you when searching a topic you've Tweeted with Twitter. For example, if you want to hire a civil engineer to work in Hong Kong, include "#jobs #careers #civilengineering #HongKong" in your Tweet with Twitter.

- Use Twitter's search function by entering a topic or hashtag in the search field at the top of the page; visit twitter.com/#!/search-advanced to use an advanced search option.

- Use "Reply" to respond to a Tweet with Twitter. It will connect your response to the original Tweet with Twitter, so its originator can click on the link in your response that says "in reply to @username" and know exactly what you're responding to.

- Retweet items that will be interesting so that your followers will see you as a valuable source of information.

  o Click on "Retweet" below the Tweet with Twitter, and it will be re-posted to your followers along with the username of its originator.

  o If you want to add your thoughts to a message you retweet, type your comment in the "Compose a Tweet …" field, add a space, type *"RT,"* add another space, copy and paste the Tweet with Twitter including the Twitter username of the sender, and click "Tweet."

- Designate a Tweet with Twitter as a favorite so you can refer to it later. Click on the star by "Favorite," and the Tweet with Twitter will be placed in your favorite folder; you can visit that folder from your profile page later.

- Use tools to preschedule Tweets with Twitter to be released later. *See "Schedule Tweets" above.*

- Use tools to compress Tweets with Twitter longer than 140 characters. *See "Shorten Tweets" above.*

- Use smartphone apps such as Tweetie or Twitterific for on-the-go uploading.

- Read about Tweeting with Twitter at ehow.com.

Followers. Having a Twitter account is all about attracting and retaining the right followers. This is critical and challenging, and it requires consistency and persistence. Here are some tips to get you headed in the right direction … Have fun!

- Create a concise, interesting Twitter bio that clearly tells people who you are and what you do.

- Define your target audience. Who are they, and why will they follow your organization?

- Develop a strategy for providing interesting and useful information that Twitter users will find so helpful that they retweet it.

- Monitor the daily ebb and flow of your followers.

- Track how many new followers you're adding per day by using TwitterCounter.

- Get notifications when someone unfollows you after a Tweet with Twitter by using Qwitter.

- Apply to get verified if your organization is high profile and well known so that followers can easily and quickly identify you.

- Make it a goal to get on the suggested users and popular Twitter lists.

- Link your Twitter profile to your blogs and other social networks; if you have a strong following on Facebook or LinkedIn, use it to promote your Twitter page.

- Put a Twitter icon linking to your Twitter page on your organization's website.

- Block "junk" and inappropriate followers so that influential Twitter users who check out your followers will see that you have a good following and be interested in following you.

- Acknowledge new followers by Tweeting with Twitter and thanking them for "the follow."

- Follow your competitive community to observe the size and growth of their following and to use the best of their Twitter practices.

- Increase followers by using a variety of strategies, such as:

o Keep followers interested—a bored follower will unfollow. Tweet with Twitter and retweet compelling information, organizational news, industry news, surveys, open-ended questions, Twitter tips, apps, images and links to relevant websites, social media sites, blogs, and videos so that your followers will retweet and give you more exposure. *See "Communication tips" above for more suggestions.*

o Participate in online events that use hashtags so that you get exposure to others in the event.

o Make a modest donation to a charitable organization on behalf of each new follower.

o Read *PC Magazine* to keep up on the latest trends for growing your following at www.pcmag.com.

o **$$** Consider buying followers (really!) with a resource such as www.buyrealtwitterfollowers.com or get-more-twitter-followers.com.

o Include your organization's Twitter address in your e-mail signature line.

o **$$** Use a tool like Twtify to customize your Twitter page and make it more attractive and stimulating to your followers.

Following others. Below are some tips for you to consider when following other Twitter users:

• Practice—log in to your organization's Twitter page, search for @hyrebuzz, and when you find it, click on "Follow," and you will see that you are now following hyrebuzz!

- Check your Twitter page, and you will see that it now shows you following one—congratulations! You are now following someone, and after we are notified that you are following us, we will follow you!

- Use the search box in the bar at the top of the page to find Twitter users you want to follow, as defined in your strategy (current and potential customers, members, constituents, competitors, organizations that support your industry, vendors, suppliers, contractors).

- Follow those Twitter users by electing to "Follow" them.

- Look for the verified symbol (small blue cloud with a white check symbol in the center) to the right of the Twitter page name for those who are famous so that you know you are following the right person.

- Follow Twitter users with a big following of users you want to attract as followers.

- Search on Twitter, search.twitter.com, using a particular hashtag (for example, #photography) to find and follow users who are Tweeting on Twitter about the topics of interest to you.

- Know that Twitter limits the number of people a user can follow to two thousand. Once you get to two thousand, the number of additional users you can follow is determined by a ratio based on the number of your followers to the number you are following. Unless you are famous (and we hope you do become so!) and Twitter wants you to have a massive following, your follows will be restricted by this ratio.

- Make strategic decisions about which users to follow so that you keep within the two-thousand-user limit until you build up your following.

- Add additional follow space as you need it by unfollowing Twitter users who might not fit your strategy.

Twitter career network. Twitter has a tool called "TweetMyJOBS" where you can post a job for free. TweetMyJOBS will distribute the job wherever your ideal candidates spend their time—Facebook, Twitter, mobile devices, search engines, and job aggregators like Simply Hired, Juju, Trovit, Oodle, and JustJobs. **$$** You can have TweetMyJOBS find candidates and send them directly to you or retweet jobs for a small fee.

Videos. There are more than 1,200,000 YouTube videos viewed each day ... It's clear that this is a popular medium! Leverage this powerful tool by creating YouTube videos of your CEO and employees talking about the mission, vision, strategy, and culture of your organization and their experiences working there. Embed the link on your website and social media pages to brand your organization as an employer and provider of choice.

Virtual/remote interviews. Tools like Skype, Joinme, Tinychat, and **$$** HireVue enable you to conduct live, web-based video interviews, thereby reducing and potentially eliminating travel time and costs involved with recruiting remote candidates. These tools are particularly useful when recruiting for hard-to-fill positions and large, national, and/or global recruitment campaigns.

Web-based résumé or curriculum vitae databases. If your organization does not have the money or capability to have its own résumé or curriculum vitae database, you can use free tools such as eGrabber to build a database to capture and retrieve candidate résumés or curricula vitae.

Websites. If your organization doesn't have the financial or technical resources to engage a skilled web designer to build a complex and glitzy website, there are still options. Many web hosts, like godaddy .com and myhosting.com, have a site builder, which enables you to build a website yourself at little cost. Other options are buildyoursite .com or web.com.

Widgets for social media sites. You can embed icon widgets linking to your organization's social media pages in your website, employee e-mail signature line, and in other social media pages (for example, your LinkedIn profile can include a widget pointing to your Facebook page). This will increase your organizational branding, communications, and social media connections.

Are you ready to go to the next step? First, find out how much you've learned in this section!

1. Joining _____ m_____ sites can help you market your organization.
2. True or false: An RSS feed allows you to retrieve information from other websites and embed it into your website.
3. Job posting aggregators will help you to:
   a. Share your job posting across multiple job boards with only one post.
   b. Screen out résumés of unfiltered candidates.
   c. Reduce the amount of spam in your inbox.

Answers: 1. social media; 2. true; 3. a

If you want to know more about the tools that support social media, visit us at www.hyrebuzz.com.

Applicant Tracking System

Why it is important to use in conjunction with social media

What is an applicant tracking system? An applicant tracking system, or ATS, is a database that helps you to capture, track, and manage applicant data and résumés or curricula vitae. Your applicant data is "captured" in an ATS through your organization's website, job boards, and manual uploads. Here are some of the many benefits and features of having an ATS:

- easy migration of applicant data to your ATS from job boards (e.g., Career Builder, Monster)

- automatic importing of candidate résumés or curricula vitae from your social media sites and job boards

- the ability to source candidates in your organization's prior-applicant database

- off-site encrypted résumé or curriculum vitae storage

- ability of your entire staffing team to use an ATS through a single installation

- web-based vs. client-server access to applicant data

- simultaneous posting of your e-mails, SMS texts, pages, and job announcements to your various social media sites

- reporting of candidate-recruitment activities

- tracking the progress of candidates throughout your recruitment process

- streamlined information flow and simplified communication among the stakeholders in your organization throughout the process, from the time you receive a résumé through the time you extend an offer, and beyond

- a module that enables you to offer opportunities to internal candidates before posting opportunities externally

- an interview format that supports consistency in your process

- identification of your top candidates from interview feedback as well as profile data

- post-hire performance management and talent forecasting

- reduced data entry and records duplication.

Do I need an ATS? If you don't have an ATS, you can still use social media to recruit. However, with today's distributed and global workforce, electronic society, and accelerating speed of operations, it is increasingly difficult to recruit efficiently without an ATS. **$$** If your organization cannot afford to purchase a sophisticated ATS, there are reasonably priced options available that have less functionality but still give you tools to enhance the recruitment services you provide to your internal and external customers. If you don't have an ATS, you are not being competitive within your recruitment community.

How do I get an ATS? Before you acquire an ATS, we recommend that you create a committee composed of representatives of all key stakeholders—most importantly, IT. Together, you will accomplish the following tasks that will prepare you to make the best use of an ATS:

- Establish the committee's purpose, goals, and direction.

- Develop a project plan with accountability, milestones, and timelines.

- Conduct a complete analysis of the recruitment information and communication needs of everyone in your organization—your IT resources will be *crucial* to this.

- Document your existing recruitment and hiring process thoroughly; identify all of the barriers and the challenges you face; then evaluate how you can change that process to provide the greatest efficiency, stakeholder value, and hire quality.

- Define what you would want to achieve by having an ATS and how it will help achieve the organization's goals (e.g., speed, efficiency, communication, branding, candidate quality, compliance, tracking, measurement, and reporting).

- Talk with other recruiters about the speed and ease of use, features, reliability, implementation, technical support, training, and value of various systems the recruiters have used as well as their recommendations for what would be appropriate for your needs based on the analysis you have done. We at hyrebuzz have had success using HRM Direct, but there are many systems from which to choose, depending upon your recruitment needs.

- Prepare a request for proposal (RFP) that clearly outlines the features and functionality you want and provides your committee with a roadmap that ensures you won't consider the wrong systems and features.

- Research available systems and select and send your RFP to vendors who have appropriate features and pricing.

- Work with IT to review and assess the proposals you receive, get clarification where necessary, check references, and review vendor purchase and service agreements. Invite the vendors with the best proposals to give you a presentation so that you can learn more about them, and ask questions such as these about the ATS the vendor offers:

  o Will the system meet your needs and goals?
  o Has the vendor installed their ATS in similar organizations?
  o What is their implementation process?
  o What type of training does the vendor provide?
  o What is the utility of their ongoing tech support? How is it structured? How much does it cost?
  o How often does the vendor issue upgrades, how much do those cost, what is the downtime during upgrade, and what upgrade training is provided?

- Select the vendor that presents the best option for your organization; then proceed to coordinate with your IT, purchasing, and legal experts to review and negotiate the terms of the purchasing and service agreements.

- Schedule implementation and training with the vendor, in coordination with IT, for a time that is not your peak recruitment period, and ensure that you have the proper support necessary to continue your recruitment activities during implementation.

- Expect implementation to take longer than anticipated!

It is important to select your ATS wisely to ensure that it supports your organizational goals, objectives, processes, and growth. Be guided in your selection by your list of items the ATS must have and not by extra and unnecessary features various vendors have to offer. Regardless of the ATS you use, you will realize efficiencies in your recruiting activities and achieve greater results with less.

‼ If you don't use an ATS, don't let that discourage you from establishing and using social media to recruit. Unfortunately, not having an ATS is already somewhat of a handicap, so you'll need to leverage as many resources as you can to stay ahead—and social media is absolutely indispensable.

Strategy and Policy/Guidelines

Guidance on developing a social media strategy and policy/guidelines

!! **P**utting information out into the public domain can be tricky and can lead to unintended consequences if it's not done with careful thought and preparation. We strongly recommend that you develop a strategy for using social media, not only for recruiting but also for a broad array of purposes. Without a strategy supported by key stakeholders in your organization, you will not maximize the time you spend using social media to recruit, and you'll have a hard time defending its continued use. Once your organization has agreed to a strategy, we recommend that you establish a policy or set of guidelines for the use of social media. A policy or set of guidelines will help you to maximize social media's benefits to your organization and to manage the risk of its improper use. Establishing written social media parameters may not prevent but will help to protect against the many and varied ways in which an organization can experience damage—such as to public relations, customer relations, employee relations, productivity, and reputation—or adverse consequences like litigation, hacking, information and security breaches, and system disruption.

Social media strategy. Consider these issues and recommendations when developing your employer's strategy for the use of social media:

- The goals for using social media and the strategy for achieving each goal

- The social media sites to use (e.g., Twitter, Facebook, LinkedIn, Google+) that will be most effective for your organization. Using a few strategic sites well can be more effective than using them all poorly.

- The purposes for communicating via social media (marketing, advertising, name branding, recruiting, retention, employee communication, business intelligence, public relations, research)

- Who to pursue as followers, friends, fans, and links

- How to increase followers, friends, fans, and links

- Who determines communication frequency, schedule, and content

- Who makes posts and maintains and administers sites

- How to utilize customizable features on social media sites to reach a diverse audience and thus focus and optimize efforts while avoiding discrimination. Minorities are underrepresented in social media in comparison to the broader population. Ensure that your recruitment strategies do not inadvertently pose barriers to minority candidates.

Social media policy/guidelines. Your employer should have a realistic, beneficial, implementable social media policy or set of guidelines that fits your organizational culture. It should be provided to employees during the onboarding process and updated frequently to stay current and relevant in the ever-evolving world of social media. Some experts recommend conducting training on the policy/guidelines and having employees sign policy statements and re-acknowledge their understanding on a frequent basis (e.g., quarterly). ‼ We recommend that employers not ask employees and job applicants for their social media password and access information. This is personal information and is intrusive, and a number of states in the United States have enacted laws prohibiting employers from requiring that employees and job applicants provide such information. Consider these issues and recommendations when developing the policy/guidelines:

- Explain the legal, confidentiality, and security risks (financial, strategic, R&D, trade secrets, client, business intelligence, copyright and trademark infringement, plagiarism, defamation, harassment, discrimination, litigation, regulations, and restrictions for your employer's industry) an employee's inappropriate and unauthorized use of social media can have on your employer.

- Decide whether to limit employee use of social media during the workday for personal and/or professional purposes and determine parameters for the veracity, integrity, and content of what may be posted when and where.

- Prohibit the use of social media for harassment, discrimination, derogatory comments, defamation, copyright and trademark infringement, plagiarism, extra-employment business, or employment pursuits.

- Determine your policy on monitoring and searching employee and applicant professional and personal social media pages, the extent to which their online communications are subject to oversight, the use of information on social media sites for employment-related decisions, and the avoidance of decisions based upon information that could be interpreted as discriminatory or legally impermissible (e.g., protected-class related) or that could be considered negligent hiring.

- Encourage employees to seek clarification and authorization from management about their use of social media and to report inappropriate use.

- Establish consequences for employees who violate the social media policy/guidelines.

- Designate who can use and post to social media.

- List the levels of approval required for information to be posted.

- Select which sites and tools can be used.

- Decide whether to purchase cyber insurance to protect against the financial impact of hackers and viruses.

Social Media Code of Conduct. Your employer should consider adopting an employee code of conduct that requires employees who use social media to identify what authority the employees have to "speak" on behalf of their employer, to make honest representations about their employer and the products or services and practices of the employer's competitors, and to comply with social media site posting guidelines.

Sample Guidelines for Employee and Contractor Social Media Participation. Below are sample guidelines you may wish to reference when creating your own:

Guidelines for the Use of Social Media

We recognize that our employees and contractors use social media for professional purposes, and we wish to establish clear guidelines for our employees and contractors to follow when using social networks, blogs, videos, and the like related to their work.

- Identify your real name, your role, and the name of our organization.

- Be open about your interest in and motive for what you are presenting so that others seeing it have a clear understanding of it.

- Refrain from referring to competitors, vendors, associates, members, partners, or other entities unless you have advance approval of a senior official of this organization.

- Never present false, misleading, disrespectful, offensive, personal, or litigation-related images, information, posts, messages, statements, claims, or opinions.

- Obtain permission before presenting private or internal information or discussions.

- Uphold our policies and procedures on confidentiality and proprietary information so that you protect yourself and everyone in the organization.

- Always be polite, do not engage in personal debates and antagonistic exchanges with others, and brief an official of this organization if that occurs.

- Refer inquiries from media, celebrities, and politicians to an executive of this organization.

!! Social Media Warnings

*Guarding against the risks associated
with social media*

While the potential benefits of using social media to recruit are many, there are also potential risks. Any organization that enters the world of social media stands to enhance its efforts to recruit, advertise, publicize, and market but should nevertheless be aware of the following concepts and potential pitfalls.

Cyber Insurance. According to the FBI Computer Crime Survey, www.fbi.gov, in 2005, nine out of ten companies had a computer security incident, and 64 percent of the victims suffered financial damage in excess of twenty-four thousand dollars. Part of your employer's social media strategy and policy/guidelines should be to assess the potential risk and financial damage to systems and information and determine whether the magnitude is sufficient to warrant acquiring cyber insurance ... which is now a four-hundred-million-dollar business. While having firewalls, virus protection, antispam systems, and procedures to protect passwords and prevent employees from downloading dangerous material are essential, these measures are not foolproof, and you still run the risk of claims of misappropriation of data, which can be substantial. If you have e-mail, networked computers, a website, or customer data in your computer systems, you run the risk of having to clean up after a worm or a hacker attack, which means cleaning and restoring infected files, being unable to conduct business for days, and being held liable for copyright and trademark infringement and counterfeiting. Cyber insurance will cover the cost of lost business and productivity when computer systems are rendered useless.

Discrimination. More and more governments are adopting lifestyle statutes, which restrict the consideration of off-duty activities posted on social media sites (drinking, smoking, and personal relations) when making employment-related decisions. Be aware of your government's laws when you access the social media sites of employees and candidates, when you decide what actions to take based on the information shared, and when you decide whom to connect with or block. Also, consider that disabled individuals might not have access to your social media sites and that minorities are underrepresented in social media in comparison to the broader population; therefore, your recruitment strategies might inadvertently select out disabled and minority candidates and lead to claims of discrimination.

Negligent Hiring. Be certain to consult legal counsel before you decide how to act on or react to information you find on social media sites that might lead you to believe that an employee or applicant could put your employer at risk for negligent hiring.

Hacking. If your organization's social media sites are hacked, it can result in proliferation of spam messages from the site. When this happens, you should take immediate action to change the site's password and notify your social media network. Proliferation of spam can negatively impact your employer's social media network, resulting in a lower number of connections and a detriment to its brand and image.

Endorsements. As organizations may be liable for deceptive information posted on social media sites, organizations should disclose when there is a material relationship between the endorser of products and services and the provider thereof. Organizations should also make clear to employees that masquerading as a user to endorse the employer's products and services is not permissible.

Netiquette. Your employer's successful and continued social media presence relies upon site use, maintenance, and administration. While employees may feel more relaxed when using these outlets, employees should be instructed on the rules of etiquette they are expected to follow when using social media sites on behalf of their employer, such as avoiding spam and being polite, professional, respectful, honest, and nondiscriminatory.

Confidentiality. Care should be taken to preserve and not disclose on social media sites the confidential information of the organization and its employees, contractors, vendors, affiliates, members, and customers, partners, residents, and benefactors.

Contest Legality. If your employer wants to run contests on social media sites, be sure to avoid activities that may be illegal in your area, such as gambling, and to clearly state rules, eligibility, and restrictions.

Site Monitoring. Monitor your social media connections daily and block parties deemed to be inappropriate.

You've reached the end of the handbook! You're equipped with the knowledge and tools to make social media start working for you as you recruit for your organization. All that's left to do now is to get online and start Tweeting with Twitter, friending, following, and linking! But wait—before you do, take one last quiz to see what you've retained from this section.

1. In order to eliminate being _____, you should change your
   _____.
2. True or false: Having social media policy/guidelines will protect you from lawsuits arising from employees' inappropriate postings.
3. Why should you create a social media strategy?
   a. To protect your employer from unintended conse-quences.
   b. To ensure that management values time spent on social media.
   c. To identify a clear purpose for the employer's use of social media.

Answers: 1. hacked, password; 2. false; 3. c

Conclusion

We at hyrebuzz hope that you have enjoyed our handbook and have found it helpful in using social media to recruit.

We're here to expand your recruiting versatility through training, consultation, advice, support, and other resources. If you or your colleagues want to keep expanding on what you've learned from this handbook, visit our website at www.hyrebuzz.com or e-mail us at info@hyrebuzz.com.

Glossary

Definitions of popular terms used in social media

- **aggregator:** A web-based tool that collects and delivers syndicated content.

- **backlink:** An incoming link to a website or web page, used as a primary means of web navigation. Today the significance of backlinks lies in search engine optimization (SEO).

- **blog:** A shortening of the term "web log," which refers to an electronic journal or written conversation on a website, usually generated by someone who wants to share their activities and thoughts or engage in a virtual debate. In the movie *Julie and Julia*, the character Julie writes a daily blog about her experiences as she hones her French cooking skills recipe by recipe from a Julia Child cookbook. When her blog gets discovered and gains a following, she gains notoriety. You can read and respond to someone else's blog. Each written blog entry is dated and appears in reverse chronological order.

- **blogosphere:** The totality of blogs on the Internet and the conversations taking place within that sphere.

- **blogroll:** A list of sites displayed in the sidebar of a blog, showing what the blogger reads regularly.

- **CamelCase:** Words joined without spaces with each initial letter of a word capitalized to create a hashtag. For example: #SocialMedia.

- **cloud computing:** A virtual network of shared resources, software, and information that provides computation, applications, data access, data management, and storage resources without requiring users to know the location and other details of the computing infrastructure.

- **crawling:** Using a computer program that browses the World Wide Web in a methodical, automated manner.

- **CSS:** An acronym for cascading style sheets specification, which is a computer language used to write formatting instructions. CSS tells a web browser how web page content should look in terms of layout position, alignment, width, height, and style.

- **cyberdisinhibition:** The phenomenon of net users (43 percent) feeling less inhibited online and thus behaving in ways that they wouldn't in person.

- **dynamic content:** Content that is constantly changing. Videos and animations are examples of dynamic content.

- **E-recruitment:** The use of electronic resources, particularly the Internet, to recruit.

- **FeedBurner:** A web service that allows you to enhance and refine RSS feeds. It can be used to convert blog feeds into podcast feeds or to insert advertising into RSS feeds.

- **follower:** On Twitter, if you want to read all of the Tweets with Twitter of another Twitter user, you must become a "follower" of theirs. When you "follow" a Twitter account holder, their Tweets with Twitter will post on your Twitter page, and when another Twitter account holder "follows" you, your Tweets with Twitter will appear on their Twitter page.

- **forum:** A forum or message board is an area where people from throughout the social networking community can gather to discuss just about any topic. Private groups can also use forums to promote discussions or information exchanges.

- **hashtag:** In order for you to be able to search for Tweets with Twitter about a certain subject, Tweets with Twitter have to contain a key reference word called a "hashtag." This is a word that has a hash mark as its first character, like "#socialmedia." If you searched Twitter for #socialmedia, you would see Tweets with Twitter that contain the #socialmedia hashtag.

- **HTML:** An acronym for hypertext markup language, the authoring language used to create documents on the World Wide Web. HTML defines the structure and layout of a web document by using a variety of tags and attributes.

- **link:** A person to whom you are connected via LinkedIn. You can stay connected with your links and follow their advancements and changes in professional activities.

- **Listorious:** A *great* tool for searching Twitter users on the web. You can find anyone by topic, region, or profession and interview them by asking questions over Listorious. It is powered by data from the tens of thousands of list curators.

- **lurkers:** People who read but don't contribute or add comments.

- **mega or meta search engine:** A search tool that sends your requests to several other search engines and/or databases and aggregates and displays the results in a single list according to their source.

- **mobile recruiting:** Attracting and engaging prospective talent via mobile media, communications, and technology.

- **newsreader:** An application for reading messages from syndication feeds, such as RSS.

- **open-source software:** Computer software that is available in source code form; the source code and certain other rights normally reserved for copyright holders are provided under a software license that permits users to study, change, improve, and distribute the software.

- **orphan:** An entry on *Wikipedia* that is not connected to any other Internet article or item.

- **permalink:** A type of link that will connect you to a specific post on a blog, as opposed to the blog's home page.

- **platform:** The framework or system within which tools work. It may be as broad as mobile telephony or as narrow as a piece of software that has different modules like blogs, forums, and wikis in a suite of tools.

- **plug-in:** A set of software components that adds specific abilities to a larger software application.

- **podcast:** A recording or video that you download automatically through a subscription to a website, allowing you to view or listen at your convenience.

- **post:** A message that appears on a social media site, where it can be viewed by others. Also a verb, "to post": to share on a social media site.

- **retweet:** A Tweet with Twitter you post on Twitter to share with your followers and that one of your followers then reposts to their followers. If one of your Tweets with Twitter gets retweeted, your Twitter username will appear beside it to indicate who originated the Tweet with Twitter.

- **ROI:** An acronym for return on investment. ROI is a performance measure used to evaluate the efficiency of an investment, cost versus return.

- **RSS feed:** An acronym for rich site summary, also called really simple syndication. RSS feeds allow you to subscribe to content on blogs and other social media so that you can continually receive notice of new posts via a running feed.

- **search engine:** A tool you can use to search for information on the World Wide Web and FTP servers. Google is today's most widely used search engine. When you enter a search topic, the search engine combs the Internet for sites that reference the topic and lists the web pages and files it finds in order from the most to the least precise match. Each item the search engine finds and lists is called a "hit."

- **semantic web:** An evolving development of the World Wide Web in which the meaning (semantics) of information and services on the web is defined, making it possible for the web to "understand" and satisfy the requests of people and machines to use the web content.

- **SEO:** An acronym for search engine optimization, the process of improving the visibility of a website or a web page in search engines.

- **site traffic:** The amount of visitors and visits a website receives.

- **social graph:** A graph describing relationships between individuals who are online and not relationships between individuals in the real world.

- **social media optimization:** The use of social media with the intent of attracting unique visitors to website content. SMO is one of many online methods of website optimization.

- **social networking site:** A website where users can create a profile for themselves and socialize with others using a range of social media tools, including blogs, video, images, tagging, lists of friends, forums, and messaging.

- **Sulia:** Formerly called Tlists, Sulia gives you categorized instant access to "best of the best" Tweets with Twitter from leading Tweeters, allowing you to see Tweets with Twitter from the top users in a particular category, filtered so that you only see on-topic, nonspam, nonprofane content.

- **synchronous communications:** Communications that occur in real time, like chat, audio, or video face-to-face communication.

- **tag:** A keyword in or attached to a blog post, bookmark, photograph, or other item. Tags enable you to find what you want when searching the web.

- **thread:** A strand of conversation on an e-mail list or web forum. Often defined by messages that use the same subject heading.

- **Topsy:** An application that produces a variety of metrics calculated from census-based social data sets, enabling businesses to interpret social signals in ways that are meaningful to their needs, with a high degree of precision and in real time. Topsy's technology collects massive amounts of authored content from the largest social networks and identifies the most important content seconds after it has been posted to the social web.

- **Tweet:** A message posted on Twitter by a Twitter account holder. Tweets with Twitter have a 140-character limit.

- **Twitter abbreviated words:**
  o **b/c** = because
  o **BFN** = bye for now
  o **BG** = background (specifically, a user's Twitter background page)
  o **BR** = best regards
  o **BTW** = by the way
  o **DM** = direct message
  o **EM** = e-mail
  o **FB** = Facebook
  o **FTF** = face-to-face
  o **FWIW** = for what it's worth
  o **Gr8** = great
  o **IMHO** = in my honest opinion or in my humble opinion
  o **IMO** = in my opinion
  o **IRL** = in real life
  o **J/K** = just kidding
  o **LI** = LinkedIn
  o **LMAO** = laughing my ass off
  o **LMBO** = laughing my butt off
  o **LMK** = let me know
  o **LOL** = laughing out loud
  o **NP** = no problem

- o **OMFG** = oh my f—ing God
- o **OMG** = oh my God
- o **PLZ** = please
- o **ROFL** = rolling on the floor laughing
- o **RT** = retweet
- o **RTHX** = thanks for the retweet
- o **TMB** = Tweet me back
- o **TMI** = too much information
- o **TTYL** = talk to you later
- o **TTYS** = talk to you soon
- o **TY** = thank you
- o **WTF** = what the f—
- o **WTH** = what the heck
- o **YW** = you're welcome
- o **<3** = the text version of a heart

- **Voice Over Internet Protocol:** With VOIP, you can use a computer to place phone calls without additional charge, including conference calls. VOIP does not require that you use a telephone—one popular and common VOIP tool is Skype.

- **Web 2.0:** Commonly associated with web applications that facilitate interactive information sharing, interoperability, user-centered design, and collaboration on the World Wide Web. A Web 2.0 site allows users to interact and collaborate with each other in a social media dialogue as creators (prosumers) of user-generated content in a virtual community, in contrast to websites where users (consumers) are limited to the passive viewing of content that was created for them. Examples of Web 2.0 include social networking sites, blogs, wikis, video-sharing sites, hosted services, web applications, mashups, and folksonomies.

- **widget:** A stand-alone application that you can embed in a website, desktop, or mobile phone that can help you search or quickly and easily access websites and information.

- **XML:** An acronym for extensible markup language, which is a set of rules for encoding documents in a machine-readable form, like html. XML formats documents to be simple and usable over the Internet.